# Writing Your First Book Made Easy

## Volume 1

Luther T. Collins

Printed in the United States of America

Published: by Legacy Voice Productions

Copyright © 2021 by Luther T. Collins

All rights reserved. This book or parts thereof may not be reproduced in any form, stored in a retrieval system, or transmitted in any form by any means- electronic, mechanical, photocopy, recording, or otherwise-without prior written permission of the author, except as provided by United States of America copyright law.

Cover Design by: Javeria Saleem

ISBN: 978-1-7351253-4-3

To contact author for booking or ordering additional copies, go to: legacyvoiceproductions@gmail.com

## Table of Contents

Intro

Chapter 1 - Just Write

Chapter 2 – Turning Your Works into a Book

Chapter 3 – Structure

Chapter 4 – The Title of Your Book

Chapter 5 – Set Up Your Book

Chapter 6 – Book Cover

Chapter 7 – Book Publishing

## Intro

This book was created for those individuals who desire to take the next step in the book writing process. I'm a firm believer that everyone has their very own story to tell. But not everyone knows how to start the process.

Let this book be your guide to beginning the process of book writing.

## Chapter 1 - Just Write

*Never sell yourself short for everyone has a story to tell. Nobody has the same story. Your story can be life related, fiction, nonfiction, self-help, or whatever you decide but just remember it's your story. This is what makes you unique and sets you apart from everyone else.*

*In most cases some individuals never get to tell their story because they don't know how. When you have never written before the question remains where* do I start. The answer to this question is in your writing. If you never began writing you will never release your works on the inside.

Think back to when you were in school and your teacher gave you a writing assignment to complete. Not every assignment was an easy task. As a matter of fact sometimes you get those projects that you don't know how you're going to complete. But when you get started you've already completed half of the battle.

When writing your book or telling your story the first key is to just write. Begin writing everything that comes to you directly and indirectly. Even when the times are inconvenient you still have to write.

Sometimes you may have to pull over to jot down some notes. Sometimes you may have to break out the tape recorder or cell phone and record your notes. Sometimes you may have to go in the bathroom and write. Sometimes you may you may have to wake up in the middle of the night to write.

*No matter what obstacles you face you must continue to write. Obstacles are just objectives waiting to be achieved over time. This is why it's so important that you don't let right now thoughts escape your mind. Always write and record things right then and there on the spot.*

*Never allow writers block to even enter your circle. Change your environment or change your subject. Keep writing until something happens no matter what.*

Writing is good therapy and also your release. The paper does not talk back when you write. In fact, paper is the best listener because it records your writings. When you have things on your chest you can write until it clears your mind. Writing will free you if you allow it to work for you.

Everything starts with writing. Your stories, your words, your works, and your experiences are all waiting to be written. Let your legacy live on forever through your writings. This is your chance to introduce *yourself to the world by just writing.*

## Chapter 2 – Turning Your Works into a Book

*Most people never think of writing a book because they think it's too hard or requires extensive work. The truth is you don't have to have a degree in writing or be a scholar to write a book. Believe it or not it's not as hard as you think it may be.*

*Once you have completed the writing process than it's all about making a decision. By taking this step you have decided that I have a story to tell that I want to share with the world.*

*In taking this step it's always recommended to do your homework. This is where you read, research, and reach out to those who have gone before you in this process. Find out what all it entails. You want to know all minor as well as major details in this process.*

*Since writing a book is not an overnight thing you must understand it's a process. While you can wake up one day and say I want to write a book. However you cannot rush the process in the creation of the book.*

*You should always keep your writings a secret. By this I mean you don't share your finished or unfinished works without first copywriting them. If you share your works prematurely you unknowingly give others your permission to steal your hard work.*

*Turning your works into a book is releasing your vision and your voice. Your book should have value for the reader. Your book is a mini representation of you, how will you present yourself?*

Never let the fear of the unknown prevent you from writing and releasing your story. Some of the greatest writers of the world were in your shoes once. Could you image yourself writing a bestselling book?

Well it will never happen if you never make a decision to begin the process. Please keep in mind that not every author will be successful but if you never attempt the process you will never enter the conversation.

Share your journey and tell your story. The world is

*waiting for your words to come to the surface. The feeling of holding your book for the first time is beyond expression. Stop waiting and start the process today.*

*By turning your works into a book you give your vision a voice. You can be responsible for that laughter, those tears, that relaxation, that enjoyment, and so much more. A book is a powerful tool that provides inspiration, provides wisdom, provides entertainment, provides knowledge, and so much more.*

## Chapter 3 – Structure

Now that you said yes it's time to establish structure. Your book arrangement consists of the construction, formation, and shape. If you have no strategy or game plan as it relates to your book structure than you are setting yourself up for failure. Through good structure you can write your book as you go.

For first time writers I highly recommend a table of contents depending on the book you are writing as this is one of the easiest ways to create a simple layout. This is not a must have as some books are actually better without a table of contents. This is something you will determine as you began your structure process.

For every book in the beginning process it's a good idea to first write a synopsis of what you want to talk about in the book. By doing this you give yourself a basic outline to follow. This will also keep you on topic as you always want to stick to the script.

When you do utilize the table of contents you determine what you want to talk about for each chapter. So you should have a general synopsis of the book and several mini ones for each chapter. Then you begin the sorting of your writing process.

Let's look at an example for a book about hotdogs.

Chapter 1 - Boiling Hotdogs (My strategy and secret recipe for boiling hotdogs synopsis)

Chapter 2 - Fried Hotdogs (My strategy and secret

*recipe for fried hotdogs synopsis)*

*Chapter 3 - Grilled Hotdogs (My strategy and secret recipe for grilled hotdogs synopsis)*

*My initial synopsis would talk about the different ways of cooking hotdogs. And then for each chapter I would have a mini synopsis (about a paragraph long or so) for each specific chapter. Then I would go back to my writings, notes, and recordings and plug them into their respective places. However, not every note,* recording, or writing will fit into your book.

Just remember your structure is your layout or foundation of your book. Your structure should always make for easy reading and simple navigation. You never want to skip the structure part for your book. You determine the book flow by how you structure your book.

An example of this would be if you remove the structure from a house, than you have no foundation. Without a foundation your home *becomes a danger zone. The foundation holds everything together just as it does for your book.*

*There is no specific strategy for your books structure. Creativity is always welcome as sometimes you have to go outside the box and make your book unique. A book without structure is like a television show without a title, a song without a hook, or a pen without the paper.*

## Chapter 4 – The Title of Your Book

Now we've made it to the fun and creative part of the book writing process. Now that we have written and structured the book accordingly we have to find a title. This is one of the most important parts of your book.

The title needs to be something catchy, unique, and a representation of your work. When people see your book title they should have an idea of what the book is about. Yet at the same time *you want it to capture their attention. If your book title does not make someone say that sounds interesting you may want to go back to the drawing board.*

*A good cheat sheet for determining how to title your book is search for words and phrases that describe your book. If your book is writing styles than you would jot down the different writing styles:*

*Ex. expository, descriptive, persuasive, and narrative*

*Next you would write down descriptive words that*

describe these writing styles like:

Creative, unique, graphic, expressive, illustrative, vivid, cogent, effective, influential, descriptive, hermeneutic, story, chronicle, history, and portrayal

Next you play around with ideas by attaching names:

Creative Writing Styles

Unique Writing Styles

Styles of Writing

Revealing Styles of Writing

*Remember there is no right or wrong way to title your book. Sometimes you have to dare to be different. Never be afraid to go outside of the box for your book title. Remember this may make the difference if someone decides to read your book or not.*

*Other ways to create a unique book title is to search for similar books online, at the book store, at the library, or around the house for ideas only. Also ask close friends, family members, teachers, mentors, advisors, etc. for input and don't be afraid to bounce ideas off of them.*

*Definitely wouldn't recommend allowing someone else outside of a spouse or child to name your book as they may want the credit for the title for themselves. Always use your own discretion when making these decisions. And remember to keep quiet until your book is ready for release, it's a secret.*

## Chapter 5 – Set Up Your Book

Setting your book up is a very fun part of the process as well. This is where you put your stamp of DNA on your work. Remember you are the author and organizer of this work.

So you have written your book, you have structured your book, and you have titled your book. Now it's time to ensure you have everything in place to prepare your book for printing. The setting up process is where you can see your works as an actual book being formed.

In setting your book up you want to determine the exact order or flow. The structure and the set up are similar but different as it relates to your book. While the structure is used to help you write the book the set up is used to help you with the actual layout of the book.

The set up usually happens after you write the book because it consists of your add-ons or takeaways. For instance if you need to increase or decrease your *page number's you can do so at this point. These items are typically not as important as writing the book and that's why it's a good idea to do this at the end so it won't be a distraction.*

*Some of the things you will determine at this point are if you choose to have a dedication page, intro page, acknowledgements, foreword page, promotional pages, upcoming events page, etc. Always keep in mind that this is your book and your set up. While it's always useful to get ideas, creativity is the key.*

*Now that we have written the book and titled the book we are ready to set up the book:*

*Foreword*

*Intro*

*Special Acknowledgements*

*Table of Contents*

*Chapter 1*

*Chapter 2*

*Chapter 3*

*Final Thoughts*

*In this example we have set up the book. Once you have initialized your set up than you have to go through each individual section and ensure everything is properly in place. During this process your dedication to the set up can determine your books destination.*

*The set up is a very important part of the process. You want it to make sense and flow smoothly for the reader. It does not have to mirror other books unless you choose to do so.*

*Great job, my friend you have just completed your very own book set up.*

## Chapter 6 – Book Cover

The book cover and the title equally consist of the most important parts of the book. If your book cover does not match the title, it can only be a recipe for disaster. Your book cover should embody your title as well as your inner works or writings.

Some questions you should ask yourself. What do you want your cover to say about your book? Is there a specific color theme for your book? What kind of books do you buy? Why do you buy them?

*Remember long before people ever pick up your book to read they will first see your cover and title. The words in your book are just a byproduct of the outside makeup. Always ask for direct and honest feedback as it relates to your cover.*

*Your book cover should be held to the same regard as your inner works. If you just focus on writing the book and neglect the book cover process you may limit your sales to the minimum. If your book cover is not captivating it may easily get overlooked.*

*Don't be a copycat but be a creative. If you use similar books for ideas, use them for just that. Never duplicate someone else's cover as this is your opportunity to show the world your own innovative talent.*

*If you are not a graphic designer as most people are not than search until you find that person that is able to capture your vision. Book covers can be expensive but there are other resources (which even includes doing them yourself online) for affordable covers. Just make sure that you don't sacrifice the quality or content as you prepare to display your cover.*

*Give yourself options as it relates to your book cover idea. For example if your book is about cell phones:*

- *Do a new iphone design*
- *Do a new android design*
- *Do a multiple phone design*
- *Do a versus phone design*
- *Do a flip phone design*
- *Create a futuristic cell phone that doesn't exist as a design*

Now that you have given yourself options you have to vote. First you pick the one you like best. Then you find a small panel of friends, family, and associates to help out. Next let them vote for their favorite.

Keep in mind the cover must reflect the content in the container of your book. Give your audience the full experience inside and out. Let your book cover be the light that ignites the fire in your book.

## Chapter 7 - Book Publishing

Congratulations on writing your book. As you can see, it's really not as hard as you thought it would be. However finding the right publishing process will require some research.

You always have the option of self publishing. If you do decide to self publish on your own there are a variety of different companies that will allow you to utilize their capabilities if you choose to do so. Selecting this route simply means you have to do all of the leg work. But in return they can be your print on demand station, book supplier, and distribution center depending on the services they offer.

The good news is that this is not the only option as some individuals may not be comfortable with this process. Some individuals may not have the time to invest in this process. And some may not have the computer skills or access to complete the book publishing process on their own.

*Another option is publishing through a self publishing company. This requires spending various amounts of money. Some publishers charge a lot and some charge a little depending on the various packages offered. Please do your research as not everyone is integral when it comes to this process.*

*Another option is submitting your works to a publishing company in hopes of receiving a traditional or even partial publishing contract. While this is like winning the lottery it's* definitely not out of the question. You have to do your research to find out who is accepting submissions, what kind of submissions they are accepting, and how to send your submission.

Do not let this process discourage you. Please, please, please do your research, ask questions, and seek wisdom from successful authors. Research should always start with reading books that specialize in this area. There are support groups on social media that can be very helpful as well.

*Remember there are others who have already done this process and became successful. Never be afraid to reach out to someone else. If you don't get the answer you desire than keep researching and reaching out until you do.*

*If you took the time required to write the book, then you have already completed over half of the battle. The publishing process is a very small but detailed part of the process compared to writing the book.*

*In closing please have your works edited and copyrighted. Find professionals in these areas and be selective in your publishing process. Most publishers offer these services but keep in mind that not everyone values your work as much as you do. Choosing the wrong publisher can take the joy out of the writing process so choose wisely.*

*Much success to you and big Congrats on becoming a New Author!*

## Final Thoughts

Thank you for purchasing this book as I don't take it lightly or for granted. I hope this book has been helpful in your writing process. Please share what you've learned as knowledge is power and wisdom is a tool when applied.

God gave me this book to help those who desire to write but may not know where to start. During my writing journey I experienced a lot of defeat mostly in the publishing process. I spent a lot of money and received very little to nothing in return utilizing multiple publishers.

*I have learned a lot from my mistakes and turned my miscues into a platform to help others in need. This may not be for everyone but we are here for those in need. Please reach out if you're ready to make your vision your voice and give your legacy the opportunity to become legendary.*

*Legacy Voice the small publisher with the big heart!*

*Contact us today for your free consultation and a step by step walk through of the writing process!*

*Publishing for selected authors only at an affordable price!*

*We include a book cover, an ISBN number, and a distribution channel at unbelievably affordable prices!*

*legacyvoiceproductions@gmail.com*